Table of Contents

Chapter 1

Five steps

1.1 Download

The necessary software is a simple text editor and Java in a version that runs the code to be working inside this book. We will recommend any text editor and Java SE Development Kit in version 8u101. The text editor used in this book is Vim. It is possible do the download from http://www.vim.org/download.php.

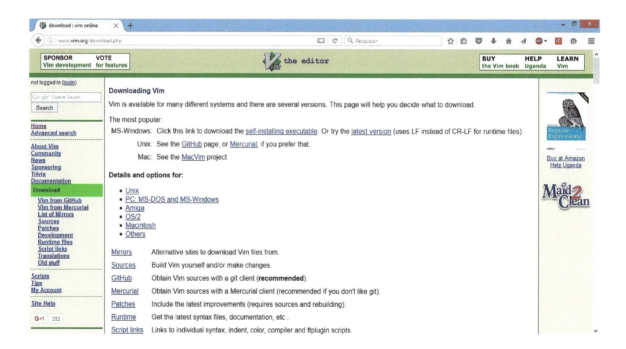

The Java SE Development Kit in version 8u101 must be downloaded from http://www.oracle.com/technetwork/java/javase/downloads/jdk8-downloads-

2133151.html?ssSourceSiteId=otnpt. Attention to choose the version accordingly to your operational system and to accept License Agreement.

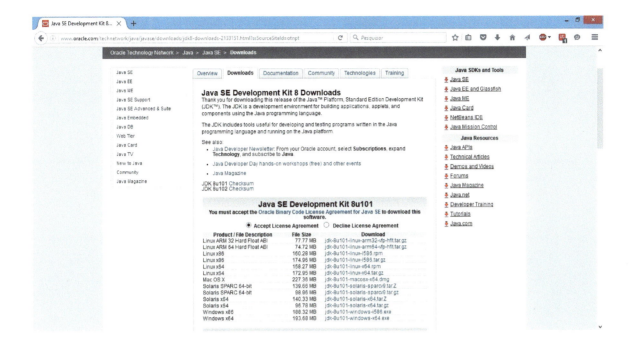

1.2 Install

First, install Vim. It is very simple. See the figures below:

Click on the button "I Agree".

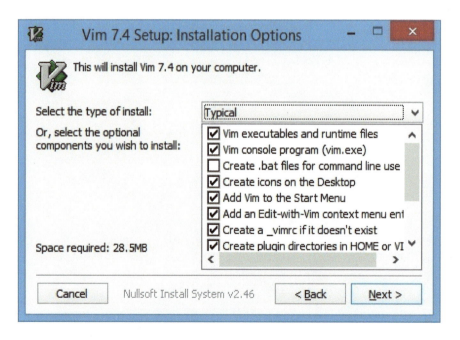

Click on the button "Next".

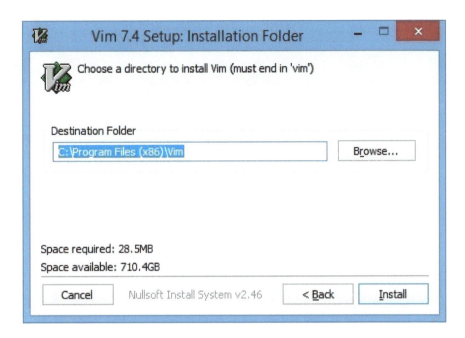

Choose the destination folder. Normally, it is possible use the suggestion. Then, click Install.

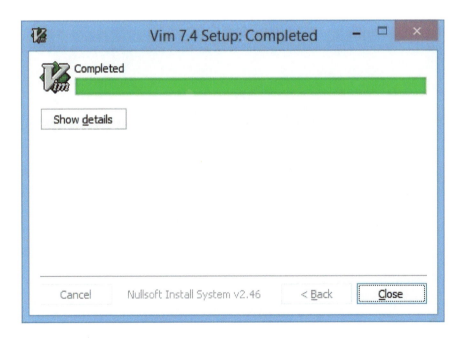

Finally, install Java SE Development Kit 8 Update 101 or more recent. After download the software from site and click on the downloaded file, a window will open:

Click Next and the installation will start:

Click Next again and a new window will open:

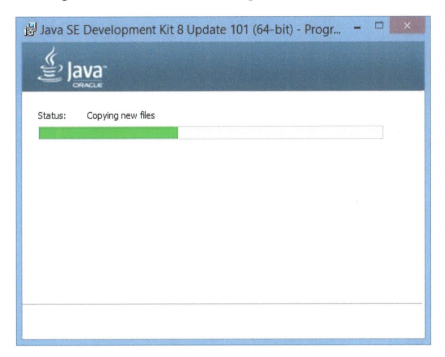

Click Next and see the Java Installation:

Finally, the message below appears:

1.3 Write the code

Open the text editor and write the code below:

```
import javafx.application.*;

import javafx.beans.value.*;

import javafx.collections.*;

import javafx.collections.ListChangeListener.*;

import javafx.concurrent.Worker.*;

import javafx.event.*;

import javafx.geometry.*;

import javafx.scene.*;

import javafx.scene.control.*;

import javafx.scene.image.*;

import javafx.scene.layout.*;

import javafx.scene.paint.*;

import javafx.scene.web.*;

import javafx.scene.web.WebHistory.*;

import javafx.stage.*;

import javafx.util.*;

import netscape.javascript.*;

import javax.swing.JOptionPane;



public class MyFirstBrowser extends Application {
```

```java
    private Scene scene;

    @Override
    public void start(Stage stage) {
        stage.setTitle("My First Browser");
        scene = new Scene(new Browser(), 760, 610, Color.web("#875970"));
        stage.setScene(scene);
        stage.show();
    }

    public static void main(String[] args) {
        launch(args);
    }
}
class Browser extends Region {

    private HBox toolBar;
    final TextField addressBar=new TextField();
    final ImageView selectedImage = new ImageView();
    final WebView browser = new WebView();
    final WebEngine webEngine = browser.getEngine();
    final WebView wView = new WebView();
    final ComboBox comboBox = new ComboBox();
    final Button showPrevDocument = new Button("");
```

```java
final Label historic = new Label("    Pages visited:    ");

final Button button1 = new Button("FACEBOOK");

final Button button2 = new Button("LINKEDIN");

final Button button3 = new Button("GMAIL");

final Button button4 = new Button("YAHOO");

final Button button5 = new Button("GOOGLE");

final Button button6 = new Button("WIKIPEDIA");

final Button button7 = new Button("AMAZON");

final Button button8 = new Button("YOUTUBE");

final Button button9 = new Button("TWITTER");

final Button button10 = new Button("BING");

final Button button11 = new Button("ASK");

final Button button12 = new Button("eBAY");

final Button button13 = new Button("MSN");

final Button button14 = new Button("PINTEREST");

final Button button15 = new Button("WORDPRESS");

final Button button16 = new Button("APPLE");

private boolean needDocumentationButton = false;


public Browser() {

  getStyleClass().add("browser");

  comboBox.setPrefWidth(260);

  toolBar = new HBox();

  toolBar.setAlignment(Pos.CENTER);
```

```java
toolBar.getStyleClass().add("browser-toolbar");

toolBar.getChildren().add(historic);

toolBar.getChildren().add(comboBox);

toolBar.getChildren().add(createSpacer());

toolBar.getChildren().add(button1);

toolBar.getChildren().add(button2);

toolBar.getChildren().add(button3);

toolBar.getChildren().add(button4);

toolBar.getChildren().add(button5);

toolBar.getChildren().add(button6);

toolBar.getChildren().add(button7);

toolBar.getChildren().add(button8);

toolBar.getChildren().add(button9);

toolBar.getChildren().add(button10);

toolBar.getChildren().add(button11);

toolBar.getChildren().add(button12);

toolBar.getChildren().add(button13);

toolBar.getChildren().add(button14);

toolBar.getChildren().add(button15);

toolBar.getChildren().add(button16);


button1.setOnAction(new EventHandler<ActionEvent>() {
    @Override
    public void handle(ActionEvent event) {
        webEngine.load("http://www.facebook.com");
```

```java
    }
});


button2.setOnAction(new EventHandler<ActionEvent>() {

    @Override

    public void handle(ActionEvent event) {

        webEngine.load("http://www.linkedin.com");

    }
});


button3.setOnAction(new EventHandler<ActionEvent>() {

    @Override

    public void handle(ActionEvent event) {

        webEngine.load("http://www.gmail.com");

    }
});


button4.setOnAction(new EventHandler<ActionEvent>() {

    @Override

    public void handle(ActionEvent event) {

        webEngine.load("http://www.yahoo.com");

    }
});


button5.setOnAction(new EventHandler<ActionEvent>() {
```

```
        @Override

        public void handle(ActionEvent event) {

            webEngine.load("http://www.google.com");

        }

    });



    button6.setOnAction(new EventHandler<ActionEvent>() {

        @Override

        public void handle(ActionEvent event) {

            webEngine.load("http://www.wikipedia.com");

        }

    });



    button7.setOnAction(new EventHandler<ActionEvent>() {

        @Override

        public void handle(ActionEvent event) {

            webEngine.load("http://www.amazon.com");

        }

    });



    button8.setOnAction(new EventHandler<ActionEvent>() {

        @Override

        public void handle(ActionEvent event) {

            webEngine.load("http://www.youtube.com");

        }
```

```java
});


button9.setOnAction(new EventHandler<ActionEvent>() {

    @Override

    public void handle(ActionEvent event) {

        webEngine.load("http://www.twitter.com");

    }

});


button10.setOnAction(new EventHandler<ActionEvent>() {

    @Override

    public void handle(ActionEvent event) {

        webEngine.load("http://www.bing.com");

    }

});


button11.setOnAction(new EventHandler<ActionEvent>() {

    @Override

    public void handle(ActionEvent event) {

        webEngine.load("http://www.ask.com");

    }

});


button12.setOnAction(new EventHandler<ActionEvent>() {

    @Override
```

```java
    public void handle(ActionEvent event) {

        webEngine.load("http://www.ebay.com");

    }

});


button13.setOnAction(new EventHandler<ActionEvent>() {

    @Override

    public void handle(ActionEvent event) {

        webEngine.load("http://www.msn.com");

    }

});


button14.setOnAction(new EventHandler<ActionEvent>() {

    @Override

    public void handle(ActionEvent event) {

        webEngine.load("http://www.pinterest.com");

    }

});


button15.setOnAction(new EventHandler<ActionEvent>() {

    @Override

    public void handle(ActionEvent event) {

        webEngine.load("http://www.worldpress.com");

    }

});
```

```java
button16.setOnAction(new EventHandler<ActionEvent>() {

    @Override

    public void handle(ActionEvent event) {

        webEngine.load("http://www.apple.com/trailers");

    }

});


showPrevDocument.setOnAction(new EventHandler() {

    @Override

    public void handle(Event t) {

        webEngine.load(addressBar.getText());

    }

});


webEngine.getLoadWorker().exceptionProperty().addListener(new
ChangeListener<Throwable>() {

            @Override public void changed(ObservableValue<? extends Throwable>

                    observableValue, Throwable oldException, Throwable
exception) {

                JOptionPane.showMessageDialog(null,

                    "Encountered an exception loading a page: " + exception);

            }

    });


            addressBar.setAlignment(Pos.CENTER);
```

```java
addressBar.setOnAction(new EventHandler<ActionEvent>() {

    public void handle(ActionEvent event) {
        webEngine.load(addressBar.getText());
    }
});


wView.setPrefSize(122, 82);


webEngine.setCreatePopupHandler(
    new Callback<PopupFeatures, WebEngine>() {
        @Override public WebEngine call(PopupFeatures config) {
            wView.setFontScale(0.9);
            if (!toolBar.getChildren().contains(wView)) {
                toolBar.getChildren().add(wView);
            }
            return wView.getEngine();
        }
    }
);


final WebHistory history = webEngine.getHistory();
history.getEntries().addListener(new
    ListChangeListener<WebHistory.Entry>(){
        @Override
```

```java
        public void onChanged(Change<? extends Entry> c) {

            c.next();

            for (Entry e : c.getRemoved()) {

                comboBox.getItems().remove(e.getUrl());

            }

            for (Entry e : c.getAddedSubList()) {

                comboBox.getItems().add(e.getUrl());

                addressBar.setText(e.getUrl());

            }

        }

    });


    comboBox.setOnAction(new EventHandler<ActionEvent>() {

        @Override

        public void handle(ActionEvent ev) {

            int offset =

                comboBox.getSelectionModel().getSelectedIndex()

                - history.getCurrentIndex();

            history.go(offset);

addressBar.setText(comboBox.getSelectionModel().getSelectedItem().toString());

        }

    });


    webEngine.getLoadWorker().stateProperty().addListener(
```

```java
        new ChangeListener<State>() {

          @Override

          public void changed(ObservableValue<? extends State> ov,

            State oldState, State newState) {

            toolBar.getChildren().remove(showPrevDocument);

            if (newState == State.SUCCEEDED) {

                JSObject win =

                  (JSObject) webEngine.executeScript("window");

                win.setMember("app", new JavaApp());

                if (needDocumentationButton) {

                  toolBar.getChildren().add(showPrevDocument);

                }

            }

          }

        }

      );


      addressBar.setText("http://www.youtube.com");

    webEngine.load("http://www.youtube.com");

    getChildren().setAll(addressBar,toolBar,browser);

  }



public class JavaApp {

  public void exit() {
```

```java
        Platform.exit();

    }

}


private Node createSpacer() {

    Region spacer = new Region();

    HBox.setHgrow(spacer, Priority.ALWAYS);

    return spacer;

}


@Override

protected void layoutChildren() {

    double w = getWidth();

    double h = getHeight();

    double tbHeight = toolBar.prefHeight(w);

    double tbHeight1 = addressBar.prefHeight(w);

    layoutInArea(addressBar,0,0,w,tbHeight1,0,HPos.CENTER,VPos.CENTER);

    layoutInArea(browser,0,tbHeight1,w,h-tbHeight-
tbHeight1,0,HPos.CENTER,VPos.CENTER);

    layoutInArea(toolBar,0,h-tbHeight1,w,tbHeight,0,HPos.CENTER,VPos.CENTER);

}


@Override

protected double computePrefWidth(double w) {

    return 760;
```

```
        }


    @Override

    protected double computePrefHeight(double h) {

        return 610;

    }

}
```

See below the code in a text editor:

```
                                            [No Name] + - GVIM                                    -  ⊡  ×
Arquivo  Editar  Ferramentas  Sintaxe  Buffers  Janela  Ajuda
import javafx.application.*;
import javafx.beans.value.*;
import javafx.collections.*;
import javafx.collections.ListChangeListener.*;
import javafx.concurrent.Worker.*;
import javafx.event.*;
import javafx.geometry.*;
import javafx.scene.*;
import javafx.scene.control.*;
import javafx.scene.image.*;
import javafx.scene.layout.*;
import javafx.scene.paint.*;
import javafx.scene.web.*;
import javafx.scene.web.WebHistory.*;
import javafx.stage.*;
import javafx.util.*;
import netscape.javascript.*;
import javax.swing.JOptionPane;


public class MyFirstBrowser extends Application {

    private Scene scene;

    @Override
    public void start(Stage stage) {
        stage.setTitle("My First Browser");
        scene = new Scene(new Browser(), 760, 610, Color.web("#875970"));
        stage.setScene(scene);
        stage.show();
    }

    public static void main(String[] args) {
        launch(args);
    }
}
class Browser extends Region {

    private HBox toolBar;

                                                            19,0-1          Top
```

Now save the code with exactly this name: MyFirstBrowser.java .

1.4 Compile

Remember the directory where is installed the Java SE Development Kit in version 8u101. Open a command window to compile the code saved in previous step. For example, I execute, in Windows, cmd to call the command line.

Go to directory where is the code saved. Then, write the complete address where is javac (executable file that compile java). Use one space and put the name MyFirstBrowser.java. After, click on "ENTER". Wait to compile. Use, in directory with the code, <path where is java>\javac MyFirstBrowser.java

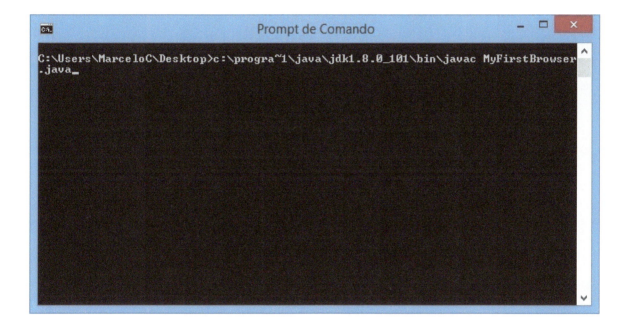

1.5 Run

Finally, use the java command to run the application. Use, in directory with the code, <path where is java>\java MyFirstBrowser . See below:

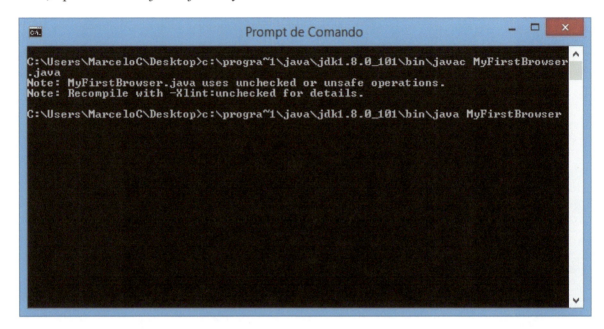

Then, the application appears:

Chapter 2

Conclusion

2.1 Incredible

It is possible write a URL and click ENTER to go to any page. Too, it is possible to know the pages visited and go to one any time. Note the buttons to more visited sites in the world. You can see videos, listen music, etc. Explore the application!

Use your first browser and compare to others. Your browser is simple and practical. The code is revealed and you can change anything to improve or adapt to your will.

2.2 Useful

It is possible to digit any URL and after click enter go to that URL. Remember to digit the protocol before the name. Example: http://www.google.com and not www.google.com .

Try running videos from youtube and other sites. If you like, tell your friends about this book and this code. Thank you! My e-mail is: mabiten@gmail.com .